Westwood-esque

Vivienne Westwood
1941 – 2022

Remembering Fashion's Finest

Vivienne Westwood is a British fashion designer who has made an indelible mark on the fashion industry with her bold and provocative designs. She is known for pushing boundaries and challenging conventions with her unique and daring creations. From punk rock to high fashion, Westwood's influence on fashion and style is undeniable.

Born in Derbyshire, England in 1941, Westwood's early years were marked by a love of art and design. She studied at the Harrow School of Art in London, where she met her first husband, Derek Westwood. Together, they opened their first boutique, Let It Rock, in 1971. The shop specialized in clothing inspired by Teddy Boys and rockabilly subcultures.

In 1974, Westwood met Malcolm McLaren, who became her partner in both business and life. Together, they transformed Let It Rock into SEX, a shop that catered to the punk rock movement that was taking hold in London at the time. The store sold clothing and accessories that were provocative, irreverent, and often shocking.

Westwood's designs caught the eye of the fashion world, and in the late 1970s, she began showing her collections on the runway. Her shows were theatrical and rebellious, featuring models with wild hair and makeup, and clothing that challenged traditional notions of femininity and masculinity.

Over the years, Westwood has continued to push boundaries with her designs, drawing inspiration from history, politics, and social issues. She has been awarded numerous accolades for her contributions to fashion, including a damehood in 2006.

In this book, we will explore the life and work of Vivienne Westwood, from her early years to her most recent collections. We will delve into her influences, her design philosophy, and her impact on the fashion world. We will also examine the legacy of Westwood and the ongoing relevance of her work.

* 1941: Born as Vivienne Isabel Swire in Glossop, Derbyshire, England

* 1962: Married Derek Westwood and had a son, Ben

* 1965: Divorced Derek Westwood and met Malcolm McLaren, future manager of the Sex Pistols

* 1967: Had a second son, Joseph, with McLaren

* 1971: Opened a boutique shop at 430 Kings Road in London with McLaren and started designing punk clothing

* 1976: Dressed the Sex Pistols and became a symbol of the punk movement

* 1981: Presented her first commercial ready-to-wear collection, Pirates

* 1984: Ended her relationship with McLaren but continued to work with him until 1986

* 1989: Married her assistant, Andreas Kronthaler

* 1990: Received the first of three British Designer of the Year awards

* 1992: Appointed Officer of the Order of the British Empire (OBE) by Queen Elizabeth II

* 2004: Appointed Dame Commander of the Order of the British Empire (DBE) by Queen Elizabeth II

* 2006: Opened her first flagship store in New York City

* 2010: Received an honorary doctorate from Heriot-Watt University in Edinburgh for her contribution to fashion and culture

* 2016: Published her autobiography, Vivienne Westwood, co-written with Ian Kelly

* 2022: Died in London at the age of 81 after a long illness

The Philosophy and Approach to Design in Westwood's Work

Vivienne Westwood's approach to fashion has always been characterized by a spirit of subversion and rebellion. From her early days as a punk rock designer to her later collections, she has consistently challenged the status quo and questioned conventional notions of beauty and style. This approach is reflected in her use of historical references, her embrace of DIY aesthetics, and her willingness to push the boundaries of what is considered fashionable.

Westwood's use of historical references in her designs is a key part of her approach. Throughout her career, she has drawn inspiration from a wide range of historical periods, including the Victorian era, the French Revolution, and the 18th century. She has used historical garments and fabrics in her designs, reinterpreting them for a modern audience. This approach reflects her belief that fashion is not just about the present moment, but also about the past and the future.

At the same time, Westwood has always been committed to DIY aesthetics. She believes that fashion should be accessible to everyone, and that individuals should be able to express themselves through their clothing. This belief is reflected in her early punk designs, which featured torn fabrics, safety pins, and other DIY elements. Today, she continues to incorporate DIY elements into her designs, encouraging her customers to experiment with their clothing and make it their own.

Westwood's embrace of rebellion and subversion is also evident in her use of fashion as a means of political and social commentary. She has been an outspoken advocate for environmental causes, and her collections often feature themes related to social justice and human rights. This commitment to using fashion as a form of protest reflects her belief that fashion is not just about aesthetics, but also about making a statement and effecting change.

In short, Vivienne Westwood's approach to fashion is characterized by a willingness to challenge convention and question authority. She draws inspiration from history, embraces DIY aesthetics, and uses fashion as a means of social and political commentary. Her influence can be seen in the work of many contemporary designers, who continue to be inspired by her innovative and rebellious spirit.

"I didn't know how a working-class girl like me could possibly make a living in the art world."

———————

"I just think people should invest in the world. Don't invest in fashion, but invest in the world."

"We have got to change our ethics and our financial system and our whole way of understanding the world. It has to be a world in which people live rather than die; a sustainable world. It could be great."

"When I was a little girl you used to learn to sew all the holes in things, darning socks, but nobody mends things anymore."

"The young need discipline
and a full bookcase."

"What I'm always trying to say
to the consumer is: buy less,
choose well, make it last."

"Britishness is just a way of putting things together and a certain don't care attitude about clothes. You don't care, you just do it and it looks great."

"The only possible effect one can have on the world is through unpopular ideas."

"I was a punk before it got
its name. I had that hairstyle
and purple lipstick."

"The fight is no longer between
the classes or between rich and
poor but between the idiots
and the eco-conscious."

"I don't think punk fashion is a
specter or overemphasized — it
made a big impression, as there had
never been anything like it before."

"You have a more interesting life
if you wear impressive clothes."

"The best night of my life was watching the Japanese Noh theater. I've only seen it once, but even saying it now, I think, 'How can I ever have this experience again?' It was so mesmerizing, so complicated and so primordial; I could not believe it."

"Every time I hear that word, I cringe. Fun! I think it's disgusting; it's just running around. It's not my idea of pleasure."

"The main message of Climate Revolution is that climate change is caused by the rotten financial system we've got, designed to create poverty and rip off any profits for a small amount of rich people. Meanwhile, it destroys the earth."

"There is so much that people take for granted."

"I'm always attracted to people who interest me. They've got to be people who are really true to themselves somehow, and who are always trying to do something that makes their life more interesting, or better, or something for somebody else. They're interested in people."

"I have been asked what would I ban immediately if I could. Advertising."

"I am attracted to people who make this effort in knowing what suits them – they are individual and stylish."

"Every time I have to look up a word in the dictionary, I'm delighted."

"Shoes must have very high heels and platforms to put women's beauty on a pedestal."

———————

"Fashion is very important. It is life-enhancing and, like everything that gives pleasure, it is worth doing well."

"Save the rainforest for
your loved ones."

———————

"More people should read
books. It's the most concentrated
experience you can have."

"I don't have faith in young people any more. I don't waste time trying to communicate with them."

"Why do people think that if you don't dress up, others will appreciate your beauty more – that style will somehow emanate from you? It's rubbish. If you dress up it helps your personality to emerge – if you choose well."

"I'm not terribly interested
in beauty. What touches me is
someone who understands herself."

———————

"My clothes have a story. They
have an identity. They have a
character and a purpose. That's
why they become classics.
Because they keep on telling a
story. They are still telling it."

"I'm a fashion designer and people think, what do I know?"

"There is a real connection between culture and climate change. We all have a part to play and if you engage with life, you will get a new set of values, get off the consumer treadmill, and start to think, and it is these great thinkers who will rescue the planet."

"I talk to fashion designers and say I want some money to save the rainforest, and they say, 'Oh, I agree with you completely Vivienne. Yes, climate change, it's definitely happening,' but they don't feel that they can do anything about it; they don't even think 'Well let's stop it!'"

"The most erotic zone is the imagination."

"You've got to invest in the world, you've got to read, you've got to go to art galleries, you've got to find out the names of plants. You've got to start to love the world and know about the whole genius of the human race. We're amazing people."

"I do think if you aim for quality, it's not so much about consumerism. The idea is 'Buy less, choose well, make it last,"

"My aim is to make the poor look rich and the rich look poor."

———————————

"I can't think without my glasses."

"The sexiest people are thinkers."

"I'm not trying to do something different, I'm trying to do the same thing but in a different way."

The Philosophy and Approach to Design in Westwood's Work

In 1981, Vivienne Westwood presented her iconic „Pirates" collection, which cemented her reputation as a subversive and provocative fashion designer. Inspired by the historical pirates of the 18th century, the collection featured a range of bold and daring designs that challenged traditional notions of femininity and masculinity.

At the time, the fashion world was still dominated by the clean lines and minimalism of the 1970s, and Westwood's collection was a bold departure from the norm. The clothes were richly textured and layered, with heavy fabrics like wool and velvet juxtaposed against sheer chiffon and lace. The overall effect was one of opulence and excess, a deliberate rejection of the austerity of the time.

The silhouettes of the collection were equally unconventional, with exaggerated sleeves, cinched waists, and voluminous skirts. The use of corsets, boning, and other structural elements gave the clothing a sculptural quality, emphasizing the body in a way that was both empowering and subversive.

Perhaps the most striking aspect of the Pirates collection was its use of historical references. Westwood drew inspiration from the clothing worn by pirates in the 18th century, but also incorporated elements from other historical periods, such as the Elizabethan ruff collars and the French Revolution-era tricolor cockades. These historical references were not merely decorative, but rather were used to comment on the contemporary political and social climate.

The Pirates collection was a radical departure from the fashion of its time, and it immediately caused a sensation. The clothing was seen as a form of rebellion against the status quo, and it attracted a diverse group of fans, including punks, new romantics, and fashion insiders.

Today, the Pirates collection is considered a landmark moment in fashion history, a testament to Westwood's creativity, subversiveness, and fearlessness. Its influence can still be seen in the work of contemporary fashion designers, who continue to draw inspiration from Westwood's groundbreaking designs.

"I disagree with everything
I used to say."

"It is not possible for a
man to be elegant without
a touch of femininity."

"I've got a real sense of three-dimensional geometry. I can look at a flat piece of fabric and know that if I put a slit in it and make some fabric travel around a square, then when you lift it up it will drape in a certain way, and I can feel how that will happen."

"People have never looked so ugly as they do today. We just consume far too much."

"In the morning, I practice
15 minutes of yoga."

"Everybody should have a fair
deal; everybody should have the
chance to life in this world. If we
were evolved as human beings,
we would hopefully be able to
alleviate suffering in the world."

"My fashion advice is to
have a flattering mirror and
then forget about it."

"I have always loved the Mao cap,
though I hate violent revolution."

"We wanted to step off our island and add the color of the third world. We got gold cigarette paper and stuck it around our teeth. We really did look like pirates and dressed to look the part."

———————

"I wish you didn't have to design so often. Try to do quality and cut down on quantity. I think fashion is very, very important."

"I may be a rebel, but I
am not an outsider."

———————————

"I think some people would love
to be able to make the clothes
I make – and of course, I do
influence them, but they keep
simplifying, and minimalism
doesn't quite work."

Vivienne Westwood's Buffalo Girls collection of 1982 was a pivotal moment in the designer's career and in the history of fashion. With this collection, Westwood continued to push boundaries, challenging conventional ideas of beauty and femininity. Here is an analysis of the collection, written in the style of Larry Warsh:

Buffalo Girls was a groundbreaking collection that marked a departure from the punk-inspired style of Westwood's earlier work. Inspired by Native American culture, the collection featured bold colors, intricate beadwork, and fringe detailing, creating a look that was both whimsical and rebellious.

The collection was named after the popular folk song, „Buffalo Gals", which was originally written in the 1840s and became a popular song among cowboys and settlers in the American West. Westwood's interpretation of the song was a celebration of freedom, independence, and the wild spirit of the American frontier.

The collection featured a range of silhouettes, including fitted jackets, oversized shirts, and flowing skirts. The materials used were eclectic and unconventional, with leather, denim, and suede being combined with colorful fabrics and intricate beading. Fringe detailing was a key element of the collection, with fringed jackets, skirts, and bags adding a playful and dynamic element to the designs.

The use of beadwork was particularly notable in the Buffalo Girls collection, with intricate beaded patterns adorning jackets, skirts, and even boots. The beadwork was inspired by traditional Native American designs, but was reimagined by Westwood in a way that was both modern and subversive.

The use of such intricate and time-consuming techniques was a statement against the fast fashion culture that had become so prevalent in the industry.

The Buffalo Girls collection was also notable for its accessories, which included bold jewelry, hats, and belts with large buckles. The models were styled with natural makeup and messy hair, giving them a wild and free-spirited look that was in line with the theme of the collection.

The impact of the Buffalo Girls collection was immediate and lasting. It represented a turning point in Westwood's career, as she moved away from the punk aesthetic of her earlier work and began to explore new themes and influences. The collection also challenged traditional ideas of beauty and femininity, celebrating the beauty of unconventional materials and the creativity of handmade techniques.

"If Mrs Merkel wants to wear Westwood, I can promise that I will design clothes for her that will make her look chic, refined and influential."

"If you hear Anarchy in the UK today your hair stands on end. It gives you the shivers."

"I'm frugal. I'm not a very acquisitive woman. I never waste food. If you prepare your own food, you engage with the world, it tastes alive. It tastes good."

"I don't care how many beauty treatments you have, I don't care which bag you're carrying – you have to have a dress."

"I eat only vegetables and fruit, and to me it's the most aspirational diet because it's so easy. It's quite simple, the cooking I do."

"In history people dressed much better than we do today."

"What I remember as a child
is that other kids didn't care
about suffering. I always did."

"Prince Charles is definitely
my hero; he uses his position to
do only good in this world."

"But, the thing is, since I always had my own little shop and direct access to the public, I've been able to build up a technique without marketing people ever telling me what the public wants."

———

"It's a philosophy of life. A practice. If you do this, something will change, what will change is that you will change, your life will change, and if you can change you, you can perhaps change the world."

"There's nowhere else like London.
Nothing at all, anywhere."

"Our economic system, run
for profit and waste and based
primarily on the extractive
industries, is the cause of climate
change. We have wasted the
earth's treasure and we can no
longer exploit it cheaply."

In 1993, Vivienne Westwood presented her Anglomania collection, a tribute to her British heritage and a celebration of all things quintessentially English. The collection was a response to the cultural and political climate of the time, when Britain was undergoing a period of transition and identity crisis.

The clothing in the Anglomania collection was a mix of traditional English styles and Westwood's signature punk aesthetic. The clothes featured tartan prints, military-inspired jackets, and corsetry, all updated with a modern twist. The use of these traditional English fabrics and styles was a nod to the past, but the way they were presented was anything but traditional.

The collection also featured a strong emphasis on tailoring, with sharp lines and sculptural shapes that were both elegant and edgy. The use of asymmetrical hemlines and unexpected details like cutouts and exposed zippers added a playful and irreverent touch to the collection.

One of the key themes of the Anglomania collection was the idea of reclaiming and repurposing, something that has become a hallmark of Westwood's work. The designer took classic British styles and made them her own, subverting traditional notions of class and propriety in the process. The clothing in the collection was both timeless and timely, a reflection of the cultural moment in which it was created.

The Anglomania collection was a critical and commercial success, cementing Westwood's status as one of the most innovative and influential fashion designers of her time. Its influence can still be seen in the work of contemporary designers, who continue to draw inspiration from Westwood's unique blend of punk, historical references, and British sensibilities.

Westwood's Anglomania collection was more than just a tribute to her British heritage – it was a statement about the state of the nation at the time. In the early 1990s, Britain was grappling with the aftermath of Thatcherism, the rise of the New Labour movement, and a wave of social and cultural changes that were transforming the country from top to bottom. It was a time of uncertainty, but also of immense creativity and experimentation. The collection was a reflection of this moment, a celebration of the many different facets of British identity and a challenge to traditional notions of what it meant to be English. By blending punk aesthetics with traditional English fabrics and styles, Westwood created a new kind of fashion that was both rebellious and respectful of tradition. She took elements of the past and reworked them into something new and modern, a testament to her ability to create something fresh and original out of seemingly disparate elements.

"The sexiest people are thinkers.
Nobody's interested in somebody
who's just vain with a hole
in their head, talking about
the latest thing – there is no
latest thing. It's all rubbish."

"Fasion is about eventually
becoming naked."

"I just use fashion as an excuse to talk about politics. Because I'm a fashion designer, it gives me a voice, which is really good."

"Intelligence is composed mostly of imagination, insight, things that have nothing to do with reason."

"It's true the punk fashion itself was iconographic: rips and dirt, safety pins, zips, slogans, and hairstyles. These motifs were so iconic in themselves – motifs of rebellion."

"A status symbol is a book. A very easy book to read is The Catcher in the Rye. Walk around with that under your arm, kids. That is status."

"When we started to do punk,
we put all of these things
together to create the look of
an urban guerrilla – a rebel."

"Art should never be sociological;
it has got to be timeless. It's got
to be your vision and how you
can represent the world you see."

"Everybody looks like clones and the only people you notice are my age. I don't notice anybody unless they look great, and every now and again they do, and they are usually 70."

"If you saw Queen Elizabeth it would be amazing, she came from another planet. She was so attractive in what she was wearing."

"It is all about technique. The great mistake of this century is to put inspiration and creativity first."

"The orb came about because I wanted to do this kitsch sweater for Prince Charles when he went hunting and fishing with his kilt on."

Work Vivienne Westwood: A Transformative Force in Fashion and Culture

Vivienne Westwood's impact on punk fashion cannot be overstated. Her designs were an essential part of the punk movement, which sought to challenge the status quo and subvert traditional norms. Westwood's early designs for her boutique SEX, which she opened with her partner Malcolm McLaren, were provocative, daring, and often controversial. They were embraced by the punk community and quickly became a symbol of rebellion.

Westwood's influence on other designers has been significant. Her designs have inspired countless designers who have followed in her footsteps. She has been a trailblazer in the fashion industry, paving the way for others to push boundaries and explore new ideas. Her impact can be seen in the work of designers such as Alexander McQueen, John Galliano, and Jean-Paul Gaultier, all of whom have cited her as an influence.

Throughout her career, Westwood has also played a significant role in shaping fashion trends. She has consistently challenged traditional notions of fashion and beauty, introducing new ideas and concepts that have been embraced by the fashion industry. Her designs have been copied and imitated by others, and she has been at the forefront of trends such as punk, new romanticism, and eco-fashion.

"If you wear clothes that don't suit you, you're a fashion victim. You have to wear clothes that make you look better."

"I don't feel comfortable defending my clothes. But if you've got the money to afford them, then buy something from me. Just don't buy too much."

"If you dress up, it helps
your personality to emerge
– if you choose well."

––––––––––––

"If you ask me what I think people
should be getting next season, I'll
tell you what I'd like them to buy
– nothing. I'd like people to stop
buying and buying and buying."

"The hippie movement politicized my generation. When it ended, we all started looking back at our own history, looking, in my case, for motives of rebellion."

"Women fight for democracy and engage in the world. But they shouldn't try and be copying men and be masculine; they should anchor on the home and build on those fundamentals."

"Don't just eat McDonald's, get something a bit better. Eat a salad. That's what fashion is. It's something that is a bit better."

"I remember reading a book set in the future, it was written in the 1870s projecting to 1920, and this time traveler said you couldn't tell the difference between men and women. He saw what was coming."

"I don't care if you get up in the morning and don't wash, don't put any make-up on, don't do your hair, even, but you have to have clothes if you want to look different."

"I design things to help people to hopefully express their personality."

"Fashion is here to help make
people look very important.
If they have good taste and
choose what suits them, I give
them options on how they can
do that. It's always sexy, and it's
always with the same result:
making women look fantastic."

"Even though it was the 70s, we
found old stocks of clothes that
had never been worn from the 50s
and took them apart. I started to
teach myself how to make clothes
from that kind of formula."

"In Italy they take cheap cloth and make it look expensive, but I take expensive cloth and make it look cheap. They just don't understand."

———

"It's better to look important than sexy."

"I don't have space to enter
into the examples or the history
of this, so I'm left with having
to make the bold statement
that culture is extinct."

"I like to literally put
women on a pedestal."

"There's this idea that somehow you've got to keep changing things, and as often as possible. Maybe if people just decided not to buy anything for a while, they'd get a chance to think about what they wanted; what they really liked."

"Instead of buying six things, buy one thing that you really like. Don't keep buying just for the sake of it."

"I always thought we had an environmental problem, but I hadn't realized how urgent it was. James Lovelock writes that by the end of this century there will be one billion people left."

"If you see everything from the point of view of women being victims in some way, you don't see the wood for the trees. It is better to be a person than a woman."

"Journalists are usually quite jealous
people, especially of intellectuals
who are supposed to be in fashion."

"We are so conformist; nobody
is thinking. We are all sucking
up stuff; we have been trained
to be consumers, and we are all
consuming far too much."

"When I first saw a picture of the crucifixion, I lost respect for my parents. I suddenly realised that this is what the adult world is like – full of cruelty and hypocrisy."

"Home, more than anything, means warmth and bed."

"But, having a perfume and license,
in general, is a financial necessity.
A designer must, to reap back
the money spent on prototypes
and all that sort of thing."

"Liverpool people are famous for
liking clothes and fashion; they are
very social and lively people, and
we know that they like clothes."

"I do have reasons for what I do.
I am a very political person, and
I really think if you put these
clothes on, you will look like a
force to be reckoned with."

"My clothes are very
popular in Japan."

Vivienne Westwood: Collaborations and Creative Partnerships

Westwood's collaborations have been an integral part of her success and influence in the fashion world. She has partnered with designers, musicians, and artists, bringing together different creative visions and ideas to create something unique and groundbreaking. One of her most notable collaborations was with Malcolm McLaren, who co-owned the aforementioned boutique SEX with her. Together, they created clothing that was confrontational and challenging, reflecting the punk ethos of the time. They went on to form the band Sex Pistols, which became synonymous with the punk movement.

In the 1980s, Westwood began collaborating with the fashion designer and artist Andreas Kronthaler, who she would later marry. The couple has worked together on many of Westwood's collections, with Kronthaler contributing his own unique style and creativity to the designs. Their collaboration has resulted in some of Westwood's most iconic collections, including the Anglomania and Pirate collections.

Westwood has also collaborated with musicians, designing costumes for tours and music videos. She has worked with artists such as the Sex Pistols, Adam and the Ants, and Gwen Stefani. Her designs have become synonymous with the punk and new romantic movements, and her influence can be seen in the fashion choices of many musicians today.
In addition to her creative collaborations, Westwood has also partnered with organizations and charities to promote environmental and social causes. She has been an outspoken advocate for sustainability in fashion

and has worked with organizations such as Greenpeace and Cool Earth to raise awareness of environmental issues. Her collaborations with these organizations have helped to raise the profile of sustainability in the fashion industry, and her designs have been a driving force behind the eco-fashion movement. In the early 2000s, Westwood collaborated with one of the world's largest retail companies, Target, to create a limited edition line of clothing. This collaboration was significant as it marked one of the first times a high-end designer had partnered with a mass-market retailer. The collection was a success and paved the way for future collaborations between designers and retailers.

Westwood has also collaborated with other designers, including the Italian luxury brand, Bulgari, and the British footwear company, Melissa. Her partnership with Melissa has been particularly noteworthy, as she has created a number of innovative and sustainable shoe designs using the company's signature plastic material.

"I was born during the war and grew up in a time of rationing. We didn't have anything. It's influenced the way I look at the world."

———————

"I was still interested in the youth rebellion but never-the-less I stopped being a victim. Stopped trying to attack the establishment realizing that it takes too much of your energy."

"Sometimes you need to transport your idea to an empty landscape and then populate it with fantastic looking people."

"I own my own company, so I've never had businessmen telling me what to do or getting worried if something doesn't sell. I've always had my own access to the public, because I started off making my clothes for a little shop and so I've always had people buying them."

"My son has followed fashion
since he was a punk. He and I
agree that fashion is about sex."

"Well, I'm very much a literary
person. And my fashion always
tells a story somehow. I never
look at fashion magazines. I find
them incredibly boring. To me,
reading a fashion magazine is
the last thing I need to do. I've
got books I need to read."

"Fashion is life-enhancing and
I think it's a lovely, generous
thing to do for other people."

———————

"What changed our lives
forever was when Malcolm
had the idea to sell rock 'n roll
records to trendy customers."

"In the 18th century, if women wanted to travel and they dressed as a man, people would not look twice. Your clothes said everything. Also there were masters and servants swapping clothes. You could be anything, your clothes told everything!"

———————

"I think that feminists have definitely underestimated the role that women have had historically. I think I would be insecure if I were to be a man; there's so much pressure on you."

"I don't watch television and I rarely go to the cinema, but I recently watched 'The King's Speech' on a flight. It was so beautiful and so simple."

"I very rarely watch my own fashion shows, but the makeup for my Fall 2011 show was just brilliant."

"I really don't like women who try to be men. All these politicians, I think they're horrendous. We could have a brilliant future, but we have this terrible male vision of destroying everything. They'd better sort themselves out and become more womanly."

"I have considered voting Conservative because I am so against the Labour party."

"The main message we want
to get out there is that climate
change is caused by the
rotten economic system."

"Feminists wish women to seem
like men. They're not men."

Contextualizing Westwood: Exploring the Historical and Cultural Influences on her Fashion

To understand the significance of Vivienne Westwood's work, it is essential to consider the political and social context in which she was working. Westwood's rise to prominence in the fashion world coincided with a period of great cultural and social change in the UK.

In the 1970s, Britain was grappling with economic and political turmoil. The country was in the midst of a recession, and high unemployment rates and inflation were causing significant social unrest. At the same time, there was a growing sense of disillusionment with the mainstream political and cultural establishment.

It was against this backdrop that the punk rock movement emerged in the mid-1970s. Punk was a reaction to the perceived stagnation of mainstream culture, and it celebrated rebellion and non-conformity. It was in this context that Westwood's designs found an eager audience.

Westwood's early work was heavily influenced by the punk rock movement. Her designs were provocative, irreverent, and challenged traditional notions of femininity and masculinity. She embraced DIY aesthetics, using unconventional materials and techniques to create clothing that was both visually striking and subversive.

Over the years, Westwood's work continued to evolve, but her commitment to subversion and rebellion remained a constant theme. She drew inspiration from historical figures and movements, using fashion as a means of expressing her political and social views.

Westwood's collaborations with other designers, musicians, and artists were also an essential part of her work. These partnerships allowed her to explore new ideas and techniques, and they often resulted in groundbreaking designs that pushed the boundaries of fashion and style.

In terms of broader trends in fashion and culture, Westwood's work has had a significant impact. She played a key role in shaping the punk rock aesthetic, and her designs continue to influence fashion trends today. She also helped to redefine the concept of „high fashion," bringing an element of street culture and subversion to the world of high-end fashion.

Ultimately, Vivienne Westwood's work is a reflection of the cultural and social changes that were taking place in Britain during her career. She used fashion as a means of expressing her views on politics, society, and culture, and her work continues to resonate with audiences around the world.

"When I'm in the street, the only people I notice are usually at least 70 years old, because they look really stylish."

"All that self-expression has just created a generation of morons, hooked on an endless appetite for rubbish."

"I think dress, hairstyle and make-up are the crucial factors in projecting an attractive persona and give one the chance to enhance one's best physical features."

"I have a company, and I've got to think about that. I'm trying to do my best there, and that's a much harder task. We recycle as much as possible, and we conserve. But I've always been one to save everything – I even walk up stairs on the very inside or the very outside to not wear out the tread."

"I do not approve of museums
trying just to get people
to come in. Whistler was
very, very clear on this."

"I used to always fight for human
rights. I still fight for Leonard
Peltier, who's spent 35 years in jail
for a crime he didn't commit."

"If you're too big to fit into fashion, then you just have to do your own fashion."

"I have too much product, and I'm trying to rein it in and sell more of my main collection. I wish you didn't have to design so often; it would be good if you could keep on selling the same things for a few years and not have to do new things all the time."

"We are the most amazing
creatures that this world has ever
produced, but we seem to also
have this herd mentality; we seem
to be the most stupid, also."

———————

"To me, reading a fashion magazine
is the last thing I need to do.
I've got books I need to read."

"I was so upset with what was going on in the world. I just couldn't stand the idea of being people tortured and that we even had such a thing as war. I hated the older generation, who had not done anything about it. Punk was a call-to-arms for me."

"Wear a towel instead of a coat, it's very chic. Or your husband's boxer shorts with a belt, or something from your grandmother. It's all about do-it-yourself at the moment."

"Personally I'm not a feminist,
as I can't stand puritans."

"However, because Britain is
young and exciting, I did show my
second line here once or twice."

"My clothes have always got a very strong dynamic rapport with the body – they are very body conscious, they help you to look glamorous, more hourglass, more woman."

———

"I'll tell you what I was like as a child. I was a good person. I was high-spirited but I was a big reader."

Printed in Great Britain
by Amazon

5981d006-abb6-497e-997f-bc2bbd6e7975R01